Celebration Of God Songs Of Praise

Inspired Writings
By
Sandra J Yearman

SERAPHIM PUBLISHING LLC

WE WILL BRING LIGHT TO ALL
THE DARK PLACES

Registered trademark-Sandra J Yearman
Seraphim Publishing
438 Water St
Cambridge, WI 53523

Produced in the United States of America
Author : Sandra J Yearman
Editor: Sandra J Yearman
Cover Design by Sandra J Yearman
Layout and design by Sandra J Yearman

Library of Congress Control Number: 2009906239
ISBN: 978-0-9815791-4-6
First Edition

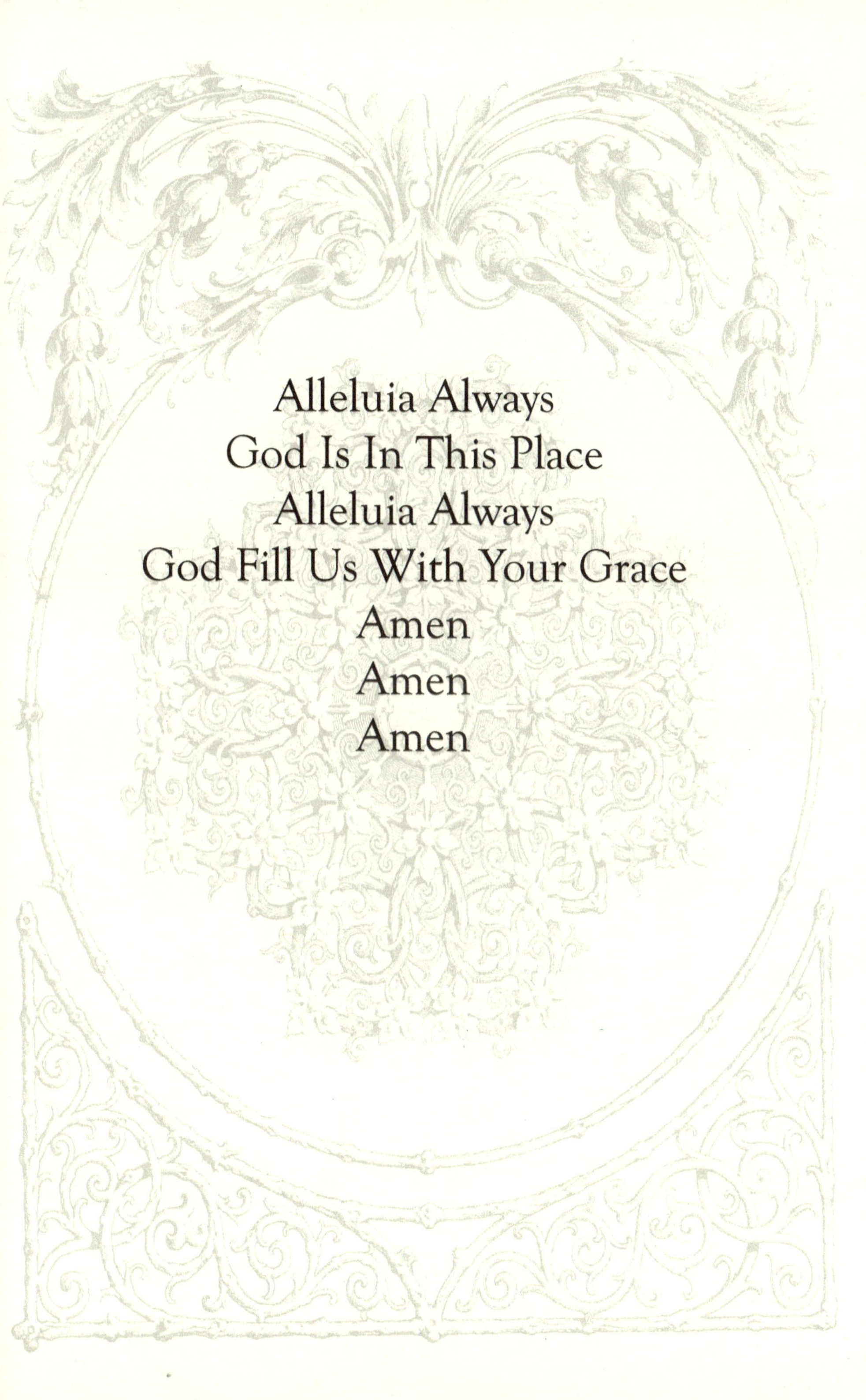

Alleluia Always
God Is In This Place
Alleluia Always
God Fill Us With Your Grace
Amen
Amen
Amen

CONTENTS

CONTENTS

Celebration Of God

All the world sing praises
For the Lord is at hand
He fills us with His Spirit
Every woman, child and man

Alleluia always
God is in this place
Alleluia always
God fill us with Your Grace

He is always near
Listen for His Voice
To feel His Presence
Is our Holy Choice

Alleluia always
God is in this place
Alleluia always
God fill us with Your Grace

I know that my Lord lives
His breath fills our worlds
His strength sustains
His Love our mantle girds

Alleluia always
God is in this place
Alleluia always
God fill us with Your Grace

God carries us always
Do not despair
Call upon His Name
His Holy Love to share

Alleluia always
God is in this place
Alleluia always
God fill us with Your Grace

Amen Amen Amen

Path Of Miracles

A Path of Miracles
A Course sent from above
A Gift from your Holy Father
To teach His children to Love

Words from the Father
Filled with Holy Grace
That conquers the worlds
All times and space

Love is eternal
Miracles from above
The Song of the Lord
Radiance and Love

Amen Amen Amen

Communion Song

I heard this Song
It made me cry
Unknown to me
I wondered why

Alleluia, Alleluia
Alleluia, Alleluia
Alleluia

Then the words of God
Flowed through me
I prayed for forgiveness
I prayed to come Home to Thee

Alleluia, Alleluia
Alleluia, Alleluia
Alleluia

The tears filled my eyes
I could not see
But I could feel
Your Song in me

Alleluia, Alleluia
Alleluia, Alleluia
Alleluia

The dark, the damned
They fell away
The Song of God
This world to stay

Alleluia, Alleluia
Alleluia, Alleluia
Alleluia

And when my life
I live again
With Love and Grace
Free from sin

Alleluia, Alleluia
Alleluia, Alleluia
Alleluia

I will understand
The state of man
The Love of God
The Lord's Right Hand

Alleluia, Alleluia
Alleluia, Alleluia
Alleluia

Amen Amen Amen

The Holy Spirit Bless

The Holy Spirit carry
The Holy Spirit Bless
The Holy Spirit lead me
Through these Holy tests

Never leave me
Never let me go
I choose to follow
Your Holiness to know

The Holy Spirit carry
The Holy Spirit Bless
The Holy Spirit lead me
Through these Holy tests

Walk with me always
Let me hear Your Voice
To worship You
Is my Holy Choice

The Holy Spirit carry
The Holy Spirit Bless
The Holy Spirit lead me
Through these Holy tests

Let me hear Your Music
Fill me with Your Song
Lead me in Righteousness
Save me from the wrong

The Holy Spirit carry
The Holy Spirit Bless
The Holy Spirit lead me
Through these Holy tests

Amen Amen Amen

I Will Sing Your Song

The Song of God consumes me
I run the Holy race
I call out to the Heavens
I seek Your Holy Face

God bless the bounty
That You send me every day
God bless the Light
That You send to show the Way

Fill me with Your Presence
Fill me with Your Grace
I call out to the Heavens
I seek Your Holy Face

I know that You Live
I have felt Your Grace
I have felt Your Presence
In the darkness of this place

I will sing Your Song forever
My life with You is a gift
I choose to leave the darkness
The world of horror and rift

I will dance to Your Music
I will take a stand
I will sing Your Song
To this world of man

Amen Amen Amen

The Unconquered Son

Sing us of Christmas
And the unconquered Son
Hallowed halls
The Presence of One

Holy and Holy
The Messiah, the All
The Sacrificial Lamb
Who stopped the great fall

Sing us of Christmas
Glad tidings, we greet
Remember the babe in the manager
We worship at His feet

Rising through the darkness
The star lit the Way
To announce the Presence
That in a manger did lay

A Life like no other
This world has yet seen
Who made us remember
The unreality of this dream

Amen Amen Amen

Little Angel Boy

Little Angel boy
Sent from above
To watch over me
With God's sweet Love

I am so lucky
I am so blessed
God please send Your Angels
To watch over the rest

My heart is so heavy
With the darkness I see
God, please send Your Angels
To bring Word of Thee

I pray to You always
I know You hear my voice
You are my Savior
You are my choice

So tonight Lord, I pray
For a fragile world
That is crumbling in chaos
We need the Angels to herald

God in Your Mercy
God in Your Love
Send us Angels and Healing
Send Blessings from above

Amen Amen Amen

A Ray Of Hope

The Love of Jesus guides me
A beacon in the night
A ray of Hope from Heaven
A ray of Heavenly Light

The Presence of Jesus
Please fill these nations
Bring us Your Peace
Your Holy celebrations

The Light of Heaven
The Son and the Star
The Deliverer from evil
Jesus we know who You are

Walk with us always
Carry us in this place
Whisper to us
Fill us with Your Grace

Amen Amen Amen

God This Heart Needs You

God this world needs You
Your Presence to some is unknown
Remind us we are Your children
The Holy seeds were sown

God this nation needs You
Our voices cry in pain
Bless us with Your Message
Our Holiness to gain

God this heart needs You
In this world run by the insane
I call out to the Heavens
Your Holy blood to stain

Amen Amen Amen

Above All

Lord, above all
It is my desire
To be blessed
With God's Holy Fire

Let me feel the warmth
Let me feel the Love
Fill me with the Grace
Sent from above

Lord, above all
It is my plea
Cleanse me with Your Holiness
Consume me with Thee

Let me feel the warmth
Let me feel the Love
Fill me with the Grace
Sent from above

Lord, above all
It is my prayer
To be with You always
To take me where

This world no longer owns me
My spirit is set free
My Home awaits in Heaven
There I will dwell with Thee

Amen Amen Amen

The Feast

The feast was kept
The bread was unleavened
The words were taught
The blessings given

The Cross adorned
With a wreath of old
The Hallowed places
Gold and stone

The rites and rituals
The prayers and lights
The Holy Spirit
To conquer the night

The Angels whisper
As the gifts are given
The Promises of God
The Blessings of Heaven

Amen Amen Amen

Precious Is My Lord

Precious is my Savior
Precious is my Lord
Who died to save me
Angel and the sword

Holy is my Father
Gracious is His Word
His Holiness I swear to
Let the Holy Spirit gird

Loving is my God
To forgive as great as He
To stand before my darkness
And save a sinner like me

Justice as from Heaven
Swiftness as the sword
Redeemer, Halleluiah
Precious is my Lord

Amen Amen Amen

The Remembrance

We celebrate Your Wisdom
Your Love and Power for
The Justice that You render
We need Your Presence more

We call for You to join us
Bring Your Light to this dark place
To forgive us and to cleanse us
To bless us with Your Grace

We celebrate Your Holiness
The Mercy that You bestow
The radiance of Heaven
The mystery that we know

The piece that we are missing
To complete the circle here
Is the Holiness of Heaven
The remembrance we hold dear

Amen Amen Amen

Pomegranates And Gold

Pomegranates and gold
Ancient rituals be told

Temples and Grace
God's Love in this place

Salvation and Kings
Holiness brings

Love without end
A Savior did send

Honor and praise
All of our days

Mercy to men
Angels did send

Pomegranates and gold
Ancient rituals be told

Amen Amen Amen

Awe

Awe is not in the trappings
And structures as we hope
Not in the garments
Not in the ropes

Awe is in the Spirit
Wherever He resides
When His Name is called upon
When He is asked to be a Guide

Men search for Holiness
In a human mirror
The Spirit can not be captured
By a world that calls to fear

Men put boundaries
On God as they desire
Instead of praying
To be consumed by Holy Fire

Awe is of the Spirit
As is Mercy and is Grace
Defined not, by a world
Bound by time and space

God in all Your Glory
Fill us with Your Awe
Consume us with Your Presence
Guide us with Your Law

Amen Amen Amen

Fire Storm

God teaches us in the Bible
He taught us with His words
The Voice that rang through ages
Through all the worlds was heard

The children realized
That with Faith they were set free
For darkness can not hold
One who has surrendered himself to
Thee

The demons were not happy
That they were exposed to the Light
When God sent down His Teachers
To bring the children from the night

Each Teacher is a gift from Heaven
To Light the Holy Course
To bring the children back
To their Father, to their Source

God sent down His Fire
To bring the Light of day
To gather all His children
Those who had gone astray

A storm He is sending
To Light the Holy Path
To teach His children
That Miracles do last

Amen Amen Amen

Shatter The Night

In all the Heavens
God's Holy Word does ring
As Choirs of Angels
With Glory, do sing

God sent from Heaven
A Light so bright
That the Presence of His Holiness
Dissolved the darkest night

Love is eternal
Love without end
God sent His Presence
To save all men

God in His Mercy
God in His Grace
Came down from Heaven
To dissolve our disgrace

The Light sent from Heaven
Will shatter the dark night
And save all God's children
Who live in fear and in fright

Amen Amen Amen

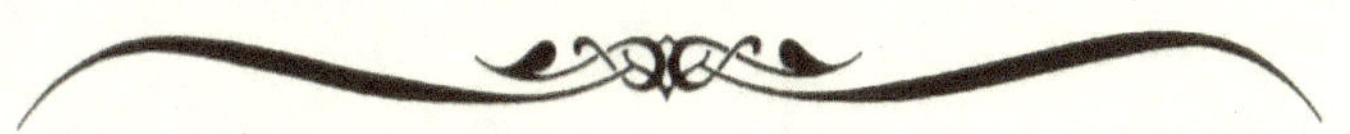

His Grace And His Love

God in Heaven
Consume us with Your Grace
Come stand before us
In the darkness of this place

Forgive us for our trespasses
Forgive us for our disgrace
Come stand before us
In the darkness of this place

A world called to Heaven
In its darkness and fear
God listens to His children
His Presence is near

God will not abandon
Those who He Loves
He sends us His Spirit
His Grace and His Love

Amen Amen Amen

Holiness Is Ringing

Holiness is ringing
This night in all the worlds
As a little Angel prays
For all God's boys and girls

Come ye little children
God blessed you this day
Surrender Him your hearts
Kneel before Him and pray

Holiness is ringing
And turning darkness into day
As God sends His Angels
To show the Holy Way

Come all ye children
Your Father is near
Call out His Name
His Voice long to hear

Holiness is ringing
In Heaven and below
As God sends His Angels
With Holiness aglow

Amen Amen Amen

Flames

Into the dark nights
The flames of Heaven went
To teach God's children
Of the Love He sent

Every flame was a mission
Every flame was a star
To shine through the darkness
Both near and afar

The flames went with God's Blessings
They sang the Holy Song
To protect all God's children
And to teach of the wrong

And into the darkness
God's Angels went
To save all His children
The Love that He sent

Amen Amen Amen

A Radiant Gift

A child born in a manger
A radiant Gift sent here
A star lit up the entire world
To announce that God was near

The animals grew quiet
The shepherds struck with awe
By a message sent from Heaven
By the star that they saw

Kings travelled forward
From the corners of the worlds
Captivated by the Light
And the Song the Angels herald

Bow, they did before Him
The babe in swaddling clothes
The world never realized
The Blessings God bestowed

On this night our world changed
The realities that we know
The world never realized
The Blessings God bestowed

Amen Amen Amen

What Strength We Have

All the things we rescue
All the things we grieve
What are our motivations
What do we believe

What paths do we determine
What paths are set by fate
Can we create a world of love
Why then a world of hate

Who is responsible for our choices
Our actions and our deeds
To whose voice do we listen
To whose voice do we heed

The poets ask the questions
The Angels sing the Song
Do the children of God realize
They can correct all the wrongs

The darkness that we call to
The illusions we create
The night that seems perpetual
Can be erased by the Holy Gate

Amen Amen Amen

Almighty Alleluia

God of all the Heavens
The Loved One we hold dear
Hear the cries of Your children
It is Your Voice we long to hear

Almighty as Forever
Almighty we sing Praise
Almighty Alleluia
Until the end of days

Help us not to shriek with horror
At the paths that we have made
Help us to transcend our choices
Let Heaven come to our aid

Almighty as Forever
Almighty we sing Praise
Almighty Alleluia
Until the end of days

Sweet is the Song of Heaven
The only breath we need
Bless us with Your Presence
We glorify Your Creed

Almighty as Forever
Almighty we sing Praise
Almighty Alleluia
Until the end of days

And when this life is over
And with our Father we meet
In our Home in Heaven
On the Haloed seat

We will sing Your Praises
With Love and with gratitude
For You were always with us
You always understood

Almighty as Forever
Almighty we sing Praise
Almighty Alleluia
Until the end of days

Amen Amen Amen

A Prayer That I Request

God, a prayer that I would offer
A prayer that I request
To gather all Your children
To Your Holy Breast

God, care for those who have no others
Care for those the tempest tossed
Care for those who cry to darkness
Care for the damaged and the lost

God in all the Heavens
Have Mercy upon these worlds this day
Send Your Light to guide us
And show us the Holy Way

God in Your Hands please carry
The sinners and the Blessed
Gather all Your children
To Your Holy Breast

Feed the ones who hunger
For body and for soul
Teach us to conquer the darkness that destroys us
This is the Holy goal

Give shelter to the homeless
Let Your Love be known
Let us emulate Your kindness
Let the seeds be sown

Give us the hearts of Heaven
And clarify our sight
That we can realize the Holiness in creation
Even in the darkest night

Help us to remember
That You created all life
That it should not be sold for greed
In this world of strife

God, a prayer that I would offer
A prayer that I request
To gather all Your children
To Your Holy Breast

Amen Amen Amen

A Shepherd's Song

Lord, thank You for this journey
That my life will take
Help me to learn my lessons
Help me for Heaven's sake

I know I have a purpose
Although it is not clear
I have always heard Your Voice
I have felt Your Presence near

I would ask that You would use me
For such a task as Thee
Would send me on with Blessings
In Praises of the Holy Three

I understand I have a reason
Though this dream has not revealed
Is the purpose of my creation
To carry Your Holy Shield

Then Lord I ask to use me
To bring Your Holy Light
That I may help Your children
Find You in the night

Amen Amen Amen

There Is Always Hope, My Son

There is always hope, my son
The sun will always rise
For those who believe in Heaven
And God, who rules the skies

There is always hope, my daughter
In this world of pain
For those who believe in Jesus
An eternity to gain

There is always hope, my dear
When the darkness seems deep
Call to the Holy Spirit
The Comforter will keep

There is always hope, my child
In the chaos and the pain
Call out God's Name
The gifts of Heaven to gain

Amen Amen Amen

Be Still

Be still and know I AM God
For I will make a Way
And rescue all My children
Even in the darkest days

Be still and know I AM God
My Promises to keep
I will carry your burdens
I will dry your tears, when you weep

Be still and know I AM God
Blessings I do give
For all who believe
Eternal Life to Live

Be still and know I AM God
These words for you are meant
The Love of Heaven Lives
Through the Son to you, I sent

Amen Amen Amen

A Light Did Appear

In a time of great darkness
A Light did appear
To help God's children
Overcome their fears

To show the Pathway
To sing the Song
To spread the Word
To right the great wrongs

And in the darkness
The Light stood alone
But through the Holy Spirit
Its radiance shown

Upward and higher
The Light overcame
The darkness around it
And taught others the same

A candle can brighten
A flame can take hold
But the Fire from Heaven
Is Majesty be told

Amen Amen Amen

The Melody Will Bless

The music will come from Heaven
The music will bless our souls
The music will awaken within us
The ancient songs of old

And God has made a promise
To teach us the ancient songs
To cleanse us from the darkness
To right humanity's wrongs

The music will never waiver
The music will never end
The music will never be conquered
The Blessings that Heaven sends

We will follow the melody
Through the darkness of this place
Homeward bound and happily
Our footsteps to retrace

Amen Amen Amen

Pearls From Heaven

The Angels gaze with wonder
At the precious gifts God sends
To answer the pious prayers
Of Holiness without end

The gifts that God sends us
Are pearls within the stone
To guide us and to bless us
On our journey Home

Pearls within a circle
As stars within the sky
To light the ways before us
So that we will never die

These pearls are all connected
In a Holy Script, they say
The blessings sent from Heaven
To dissolve the darkest day

Amen Amen Amen

His Presence To Stay

They heard the Voice
They knew it not
Through ages of darkness
They had forgot

Savior and Father
Spirit and Son
Creator of all
Our lives He has won

It called and called
They did not repent
They did not accept
The blessings He sent

Savior and Father
Spirit and Son
Creator of all
Our lives He has won

Lower and lower
Into the darkness they went
They did not accept
The blessings He sent

Savior and Father
Spirit and Son
Creator of all
Our lives He has won

But in His Mercy
Forgiveness and Love
He sent His Son
To teach us of above

Savior and Father
Spirit and Son
Creator of all
Our lives He has won

To teach us, to heal us
To show us the Way
To conquer the darkness
His Presence to stay

Amen Amen Amen

Signs

I have been on a journey
The destination known
I prayed to God to help me
Find my way back Home

And while I traveled
I discovered with surprise
That many of my accomplishments
Were His guidance in disguise

I realized He gave me
Signs along the way
To help me make my choices
To turn my night into day

Amen Amen Amen

End Of Days

I am coming Home
The Path I know
From ages
Long ago

With Joy
I escape the boundaries
This world
Could never see

The Angels that surround me
I never realized
Because I could not see them
With my human eyes

Filled with warmth and radiance
The Love overwhelms me
I am dancing in the star Light
I am coming Home to Thee

Amen Amen Amen

We Celebrate

The footprints that I follow
Are messages for me
To guide me through the turmoil
And bring me back to Thee

A Song dances in the night air
Its melody is not lost
It leads me through the horror
To the Holiness I sought

The rays of Light from Heaven
The Blessings of a King
The Word that dwelt among us
All Holiness to ring

Alleluia sing the Angels
Alleluia praise be given
Alleluia, Alleluia
We celebrate in Heaven

Amen Amen Amen

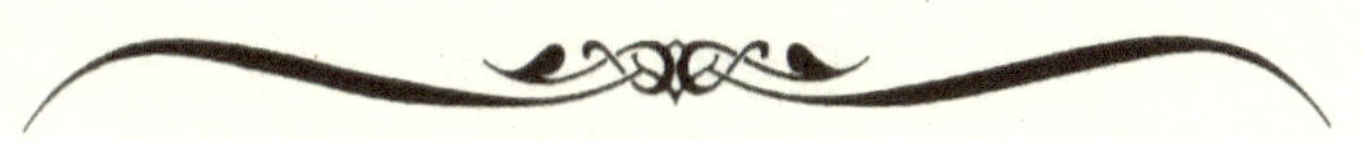

Almighty As Forever
Almighty We Sing Praise
Almighty Alleluia
Until The End Of Days
Amen
Amen
Amen

www.ingramcontent.com/pod-product-compliance
Lightning Source LLC
LaVergne TN
LVHW050942080826
845145LV00004B/1366